MAINE WOMEN
living on the land

JENNY'S MEMORIAL SIGN FOR HER SHEEP

MAINE WOMEN

living on the land

LAUREN SHAW

ESSAY BY LUCY LIPPARD

FARNSWORTH ART MUSEUM

ROCKLAND MAINE

This book was published on the occasion of the exhibition *Maine Women: Living on the Land* organized by the Farnsworth Art Museum, Rockland, Maine, on view from August 6–November 27, 2005.

Preface: Suzette McAvoy

Essay: *Figures in Their Landscapes*, by Lucy Lippard

Designer: Harrah Lord, Yellow House Studio, Rockport, Maine

Copy Editor: Elizabeth IlgenFritz, Montville, Maine

Printer: J. S. McCarthy, Augusta, Maine

ISBN 0-918749-18-2

Library of Congress Control Number: 2005928911

COVER: Jackie Lundeen, Mars Hill Triptych

BACK COVER: Sylvia Holbrook, New Vineyard Triptych

PAGE 56: St. John River

Lauren Shaw's website: laurenshaw.com

*d*EDICATION

for my father

LEITHA BY THE BIRCHES

—Contents—

Avena dog (*detail*)

Lobster Cove

PREFACE

*The land was a passion, magical in its influence upon human life.
It produced people; nothing else at all, except trees and flowers and
vegetable harvests. Life ran back and forth, land into people and
people back into land, until both were the same.*[1]

—Lura Beam, *A Maine Hamlet*

This excerpt from Lura Beam's book, *A Maine Hamlet*, expresses the interconnectedness between people and the land that is the focus of Lauren Shaw's photographic project, *Maine Women: Living on the Land*. Beam, the daughter of a Maine sea captain, spent her youth in the small downeast coastal village of Marshfield during the years 1894 to 1904. Her memoirs of this period of time evoke a portrait of a way of life that is still current in the lives of the women portrayed by Shaw. In describing her grandparents, Beam writes, "They had the taste of the past in their mouths. They lived by the weather, by whatever came, and by what they could do with the whole body."[2] This awareness of the past while experiencing the physicality of the present, is a sensibility that the ten Maine women in Shaw's project share. For them, history is a living constant, a presence that abides in their work, their communities and the land on which they live. This is not to suggest they live backward-looking lives; on the contrary, their stories told through Shaw's black and white, still photographs and video documentary tell of passionate engagement with the present and future-directed stewardship of the land. As Lucy Lippard so eloquently states in her essay for this catalogue, "Lauren Shaw offers us models of a modern life that does not have amnesia, that considers both yesterdays and tomorrows."

It has been my utmost pleasure to work with Lauren Shaw in presenting the exhibition, *Maine Women: Living on the Land*, at the Farnsworth Art Museum. Lauren's commitment to this project, her intelligence, caring attention to detail, and her unflagging energy, is a model of artistic engagement. As witnessed by the many individual supporters, who contributed funds to making this exhibition and book possible, Lauren inspires others to give as generously as she does herself. I thank each of the contributors for their part in the success of this project. I especially thank Wick and Alice Skinner, for their support through the Betterment Fund of the Maine Community Foundation. The Skinners are inspirations themselves, who give unstintingly of their time, talent and funds in support of projects and institutions they believe in, and I am grateful of their longstanding commitment to the Farnsworth Museum.

From the Museum staff, I thank Helen Fisher, Curator of Exhibitions, Angela Waldron, Registrar, Bethany Engstrom, Assistant Registrar, and Stan Klein, Preparator, for their invaluable and always professional assistance throughout the exhibition development and installation. Denise Mitchell, Education Coordinator, and David Stucky, Director of Marketing, helped to bring the exhibition to diverse audiences through the accompanying programs and marketing efforts, and were ably assisted by Volunteer and Special Events Coordinator, Nikki Dabrio-Wall in organizing the opening day events and reception. To all the museum staff and Board of Trustees, I extend a message of gratitude for their roles in supporting this exceptional

JENNY FEEDING BREAD TO HER SHEEP *(detail)*

exhibition. I also thank Victoria Woodhull, former Associate Director of the Farnsworth, for her introduction to Lauren and her work; Victoria's initial enthusiasm for the project helped lead to its fruition. Harrah Lord of Yellow House Studio is also to be commended for her thoughtful design of this book that so perfectly complements Lauren Shaw's artistic vision.

Ten Maine women of varied ages, backgrounds and ways of life, whose common thread is a strong connection to and respect for the land on which they live and make their livelihood, do not question their sense of place because they know it. Their individual stories are made known to us through Lauren Shaw's lens. The communal story her work tells is one we can all share—a better understanding of our place in the world and the relationship between all things. Shaw asks us through her photographs to be mindful, to engage, to connect. In looking at the work in this exhibition, I am reminded of a passage in Annie Dillard's, *An American Childhood*, in which she writes, "For it is not you or I that is important, neither what sort we might be nor how we came to be each where we are. What is important is anyone's coming awake and discovering a place. . . . What is important is the moment of opening a life and feeling it touch—with an electric hiss and cry—this speckled mineral sphere, our present world."[3]

Suzette Lane McAvoy
Chief Curator
Farnsworth Art Museum

1. Lura Beam, "Man and Woman," from *A Maine Hamlet*, Wilfred Funk Inc., 1957, as excerpted in *The Maine Reader*, Charles and Samuella Shain, editors, Houghton Mifflin Company, 1991, p. 298.
2. Ibid, p. 299.
3. Annie Dillard, *An American Childhood*, Harper & Row, Publishers, 1987, p. 248.

𝒫ERSONAL STATEMENT

My parents were from New England, and moved to the South before I was born. I felt like a carpetbagger growing up in Georgia, as my roots were not there, and did not belong to the community in which I spent my childhood. I felt like a visitor, imagining settling in New England someday. As I move through the middle of my life, I am still yearning for that sense of home that extends beyond the boundaries of my house and children. It is a longing for a connection that is both spiritual and real. It may

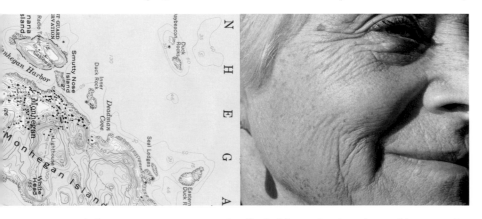

partly be a romantic notion to finally feel "completely at home," but it is also about developing a deep intimacy with a place.

Maine Women: Living on the Land celebrates the relationship between land and home. It is about what happens over time to our connection to the land we live on, the connection that creates the spirit and soul of a place. I started this project in 1996, in an attempt to understand the summer community of Belgrade, Maine, where I have spent the last twenty-six years as part-time resident, and the impact is has made on my life. It is here that I have felt a deep connection and presence. Life is simpler and affords me time to observe more attentively my community, and to contribute in ways that are meaningful to me.

At the start of this project, I began to travel throughout the state, photographing, recording, and videotaping thirty women. Ultimately, I selected ten based on their diversity in age, location, landscape, and lifestyle. I wanted to examine the idea of belonging to a place through their stories of family and community. After listening and spending time with each woman, their physical surroundings became rich in history, family, and work. I saw their environment through the viewfinder with a more informed eye. Over time, each woman understands what it has meant to live so close to the land with all of the challenges of location, weather, and economics. I have come to realize by looking at other people's landscapes, we can begin to ask and answer questions about where we live and how our space affects us and those around us.

In this body of work, I have included topographic maps in conjunction with my photographs, representing where each of the participating women lives within the context of the state of Maine. Throughout history, maps have been a way to visualize where one is or where one is going. They represent historical symbols of time and space. My photographic work for many years has been concerned with "mapping," representing on a flat surface the whole or part of an area. It first began with close-up fragments of people's faces, suggestive of a map. The lines and marks on their faces are references to who they are and what they have experienced. Theses marks reflect the stories of their lives. It has always been the stories, which are ultimately revealed, that bring this act of map-making alive. I have tried to capture these women's varied territories with a cartographer's sensibility.

The DVD that accompanies *Maine Women: Living on the Land* was created to give the viewer an opportunity to interact with each woman's landscapes and stories by hearing their voices and seeing moving images of the places that are beloved by them.

Maine Women: Living on the Land has helped me recognize the value of shared interests in maintaining the places that bind us. Year after year, in traveling hundreds of miles to visit these women, I found that each visit brought me closer to them and their stories. Coming down into South Addison and seeing Jenny's house perched at the edge of the sea, I felt connected. Being warmly greeted by Leitha at the Two Rivers Lunch in Allagash felt like I was returning home. These women have helped me understand that belonging to a place is an organic connection that changes and evolves over time. These lived experiences create personal stories, myths, and memories, which become legacies that carry meaning within the community. To these extraordinary women, I express gratitude for their friendship and inspiration.

${\mathcal A}$CKNOWLEDGMENTS

This book is dedicated to my Dad, Martin, who encouraged me to follow my dream, which was a life of photography. He so deeply loved Maine, and my warmest memories will always be of him asleep in the hammock with the sun on his face as it bounced off Great Pond. He traveled with me to meet several of these women, and shared my respect and admiration for their humility and wisdom.

Maine Women: Living on the Land evolved over ten years with enormous help and support from so many wonderful people. Needless to say, this project would have never succeeded had it not been for the generosity and warmth of these ten Maine women who opened their homes and lives to me. Their stories have been inspirational and their humility always reminds me of the true values in life.

It was my desire from the beginning of this project to reach out to a large and diverse population. The Farnsworth Museum has made that possible, and our partnership has been a rich and rewarding experience. To Victoria Woodhull who believed in this project from the beginning, Suzette McAvoy and Helen Fisher for their tireless response to my many e-mails and ever-present support, my sincere gratitude. To Harrah Lord whose talent and insight were apparent from the moment we met. To Emerson College and my colleagues of thirty-three years, I thank you all for your financial and professional support.

As a photographer, I have always worked alone. *Maine Women: Living on the Land* provided me with the opportunity to collaborate and create a community. To Lyman Smith, whose vision, good will, and professionalism continue to inspire me, I thank you for your enthusiasm, your art, and your belief in me.

It was my dream to have Lucy Lippard write the essay. I knew our paths would cross someday, but I never dreamed it would be in Maine. Thank you for understanding what this project was all about and articulating it so brilliantly. To John Woolf, who has been my digital mentor and guide through transitioning to digital printmaking, for his generosity and patience, I thank you, as well as Tom O'Brien and the Center for Digital Imaging Arts.

This book would not have been possible had it not been for the generous support and contribution of my friends and family: to Mary Virginia Swanson whose warm friendship, generous advice, and constant support have been a gift; to Augustine Blaisdell for her constant enthusiasm and love; to John Willey, guardian angel to my family; to my son Josh, the audio master, who supported me and cheered me on when I needed it the most; to Sarah, my daughter, who has taught me much through her sense of humor; to my niece, Allie Savarino, for her honesty, wisdom and generosity; and to my Mom, Sylvia, who gave me all of herself with impeccable style. It is nearly impossible to find a way to support someone who is driven by a passion that sometimes appears unreasonable—to Paul, who has always found that way and never wavered in his encouragement and faith in me.

BETTY'S GRANDSON IN THE TREE

Carol harvesting blueberries

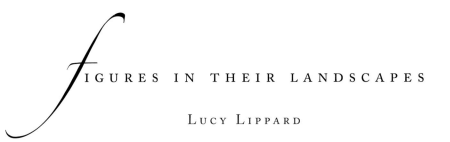

Figures in Their Landscapes

Lucy Lippard

Photographic portraits and landscapes overlaid on maps are an ideal way to express the layered attachment to place that Lauren Shaw is exploring in her *Maine Women: Living on the Land*. The ten admirable women she has selected belong here, at this point on the map. They are at home in their place, whether they are Maine's adopted daughters from "away," or generations of their families that precede them on that very spot. For others, a map is a menu for those who lust after place. For those who know the intimate details of every name, every contour line, a map is a kind of personal history. Shaw's longstanding interest in "mapping" arises from the way it translates three dimensions into two, or complex information into readable forms. She began this project by photographing close-ups of people's faces, which she saw as experiential maps. Faces also seem to reflect the furrows and changes of the landscape itself.

The names of the places where these women live offer clues to the state's long and layered history. Allagash and Monhegan are Native names. Presque Isle testifies to the French presence in the north. Cumberland, Beddington, New Vineyard, South Addison and Rockport reveal the eventually predominant English settlement. Mars Hill and Athens are classical references popular in the 19th century. The women's own names are more hermetic, suggesting French, German, Italian, Spanish, Irish, and English ancestry but made opaque by marriages and acculturation.

Lauren Shaw's commitment to this ten-year project has roots of its own. On her mother's side, she has relatives in the city of Bath and she has spent twenty-six years as a part-time resident in North Belgrade. She conducted interviews for eight years, then selected the ten women shown here for "diversity in age, location, landscape, and storytelling." Shaw's work is art, not a sociological study. Although their social realities differ, most of these women are "of a certain age," and most are white. (Maine is the second whitest state in the Union, although the increasingly Latino blueberry pickers and farm workers are probably not counted in the population.) Shaw has chosen to focus, as in a still portrait, on the person as she presents herself. In both the photographic triptychs and the accompanying DVD, the women's own voices highlight the narrative continuity of the land on which their lives are open-ended chapters. It becomes clear that belonging to a place can be a hard bargain. It means you are in its clutches. It won't let you go. It haunts your dreams and memories even (or especially) if you have been there "forever," and almost take it for granted.

The tranquility of Shaw's images convey parochial knowledge and a disappearing more innocent way of life, informed nevertheless by joys and hardships. Each landscape is a living social space, carved out of a wider series of possibilities, ultimately formed by global events and local powers. Shaw composed through a series of poignant glimpses, with images, words, and implied connections. Esthetic surprises appear now and then in the DVD. For instance, a vibrant green tree is centered in a black-and-white landscape, and her occasional use of slow motion is a theatrical device, eerily suggesting the timelessness of the relationship between women and land.

If we know Maine at all, we can sense the smells and textures of those places, but there are in fact many Maines. These portraits give us tastes of regions out of sight, hidden from those of us who spend time only on the coast of the lakes and wilderness.

Outside of the southern coastal region, Maine is a poor state where life can be harsh, and it has been for some of these women. Its beauty is increasingly prey to recreational development and second homes—a historical phenomenon that began more than 150 years ago. (I have a "summer cottage" myself, now occupied by the fifth generation of our family to be annually rooted, the uprooted on Kennebec Point, in Georgetown.) Inland areas are a bit less vulnerable. Aroostook County is distant enough from population centers to be safe for a while. But as Carolyn Chute has made clear in her novels, the gobbling subdivisions are coming and their appetizers will be family farms. Cultural geographer Don Mitchell has written, "Landscape is in part a temporary consensus, a momentary solidification of the molten processes of upheaval, or a static representation of constant flux and change."

The words ecology and economics have the same Greek root, in a word associated with *home*. The stories these ten women tell and the stories they do not tell offer us a cross-section of what it is like to live on the land in Maine. Each one has a different relationship to the land she loves and lives with. But one thing is the same: they understand where they are. For those who don't think land-based people appreciate the esthetics of their surroundings, listen to Sylvia Holbrook: "I've always loved the country. You can see for miles and miles. It's beautiful. When the leaves turn in the fall, I go out and sit in the truck and just look and look."

Mary Philbrook, the first female Micmac chief, from among the first peoples to be land-based in what is now Maine, lives in Presque Isle (I once lived there for a couple of winter months, snowshoeing over the buried potato fields, knowing little else about what lay beneath.) The Micmac have adopted Pan-Indian customs from the western Plains Natives—teepees, powwows, sweat lodges and war bonnets. But the northern forests are their identity. "This is part of me. This is who I am," says Philbrook, advocating respect for all things, giving thanks, and avoiding "outside negative forces."

Community (and lack thereof) is a major part of place. In fact, a place without history, memory, and community is two-dimensional in the flattest sense. It becomes the "site" of whatever is next to be imposed upon it. Farming communities have changed in our lifetimes. Though these women are Yankees, not given to complaining, a refrain echoes through the elders' stories. "Farmers used to help each other. It's not like it used to be. You're on your own," says Sylvia Holbrook, who has been producing 8,000 pounds of butter a year for over sixty years from her weather-beaten farm in New Vineyard, accompanied by many cats, chickens, cows, and a dog. At the same time, the spaces these women have created are vibrant with their owners' senses of passion and accomplishment. Betty Weir is a diversified organic farmer who raises goats and cattle and produces maple syrup in Cumberland. She jokes that she has turned down big money for her homeplace. They say, "You could live anywhere you want to," she replies," That's what I'm doing now." As she is interviewed, a little redheaded boy dashes around, climbs a tree, falls out, picks himself up and climbs again. "Self-reliance equals self-esteem," says Weir.

Jackie Lundeen's family has been farming potatoes around Mars Hill in the "wide-open spaces" of Aroostook County for three generations. Broad greens swathes of crops and rich deep furrows stretch as far as the eye can see. She has broken the "farmer's daughter" mold by becoming a State Representative. But when she comes home from Augusta, she says," I take a deep breath. Outside is where I like to be." Jenny Cirone, daughter of a light-house keeper, spent over seventy-five years as a lobster fisher up until her death in 2004, and raised sheep in South Addison. By the time she was 13, she and her father ran 145 traps. She had her own boat and license. "I tried to be a housekeeper," she says," but didn't end up that way." Leitha Kelly comes from six generations of woodsmen in the Allagash, married one, and

has raised sons who also harvest timber, although changing times mean that many young people are forced to leave to find work. She runs Two Rivers Lunch and Guiding Services at Kelly's Landing, where "I feel closest to my Mom and Dad because they walked the land here, too."

Then there are the new farmers. Carol Varin had camped in Maine with her family, married, and returned "too young and idealistic to know you can't live off the land, so we were able to pull it off." They bought burnt blueberry fields in Beddington, knowing there were "a hundred years of people before me, generations of people pickin rocks. . . . I like going places, but coming back is the best part." Raquel Boehmer lives on Monhegan Island—some twelve miles from the mainland, though the sense of distance is being cut by faster boats—and writes about food, nutrition, and foraging from the wild. "The light intensifies as it bounces off the ocean," she says. "You feel part of universal life."

Deb Soule is an herbalist who was inspired by a trip to Nepal where traditional medicine was never interrupted. She founded Avena Botanicals, an herbal apothecary in Rockport, and teaches women traditional healing practices gleaned from her ethno-botanical studies. Her domain is a series of "beautifully designed gardens watched over by sculpture from different cultures, underscoring "how incredibly necessary diversity is." Gail Edwards is the founder of Blessed Maine Herb Farm in Athens. She too teaches others to "put your hand on the flower. You must approach wild plants with a sense of respect and humility, never that you're there to *take*." Of her decision to buy land and then-abandoned house, she says, "It's like an arranged marriage. You didn't choose it but you fall deeply in love over time."

All of these stewards of the land, even those in their nineties, work hard. Their hands plunge into freezing water or damp soil; they haul buckets, drive tractors, and care for stock. Partners, children, and parents play cameo roles in Shaw's photographs, and we see only see vignettes of the landscapes—fog-bound islands, flourishing fields and fallow fields, battered outbuildings, roads into the distance, a dead moose strung up for butchering. But it is clear that these landscapes are vortexes between the cultural and the personal. All the women know that living in a place entails responsibility for it, though each expresses her commitment in a different way. They have chosen lives that are unforgivingly integrated with the land, that involve an intricate give and take expressed through daily routine, in collaboration with soil, weather, and community. Lauren Shaw offers us models of a modern life that does not have amnesia, that considers both yesterdays and tomorrows.

the Women

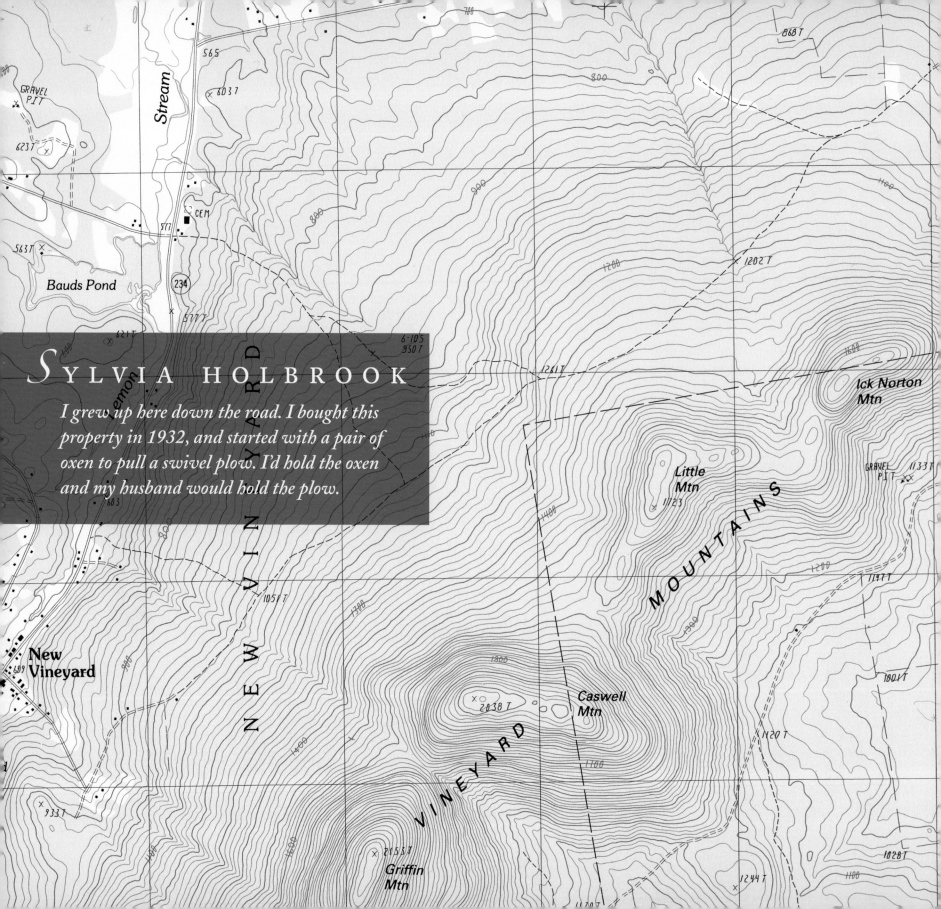

SYLVIA HOLBROOK

I grew up here down the road. I bought this property in 1932, and started with a pair of oxen to pull a swivel plow. I'd hold the oxen and my husband would hold the plow.

Sylvia lives in New Vineyard. She has been producing 8,000 pounds of butter a year for over sixty years. She started dairy farming in 1932 with her husband and a pair of oxen. She also tends strawberry, potato, and vegetable plots behind her house and is very attached to her devoted dog and cats.

"Cause I was brought up on a farm and that's where I want to be. I always loved the country. Been here ever since 1932. I was born February 26, 1915, in New Vineyard, Maine, in a house close to where I now live.

It's quiet up here. In our backfield you can just see for miles and miles everywhere, and it's beautiful. Oh, in the fall when the leaves turn, ah, you wouldn't believe it. I just go out there with the truck and look and look. Yes, it is so beautiful from up there."

SYLVIA HOLBROOK

FRONT STEPS

SYLVIA WITH HER DOG AND CATS

RIKKI BOEHMER

There is something about "islandness" that is so special. Living on a deep, water island, the land is so connected to your life.

112

213

159

60

35

5

121

129

15

Eastern
Duck Rock

60

Duck
Rocks

Daybeacon

46

21

46

12

Green
Point

Seal Ledges

130

×165

Deadman
Cove

Monhegan
Black
Head ×

×145

Inner
Duck Rock

60

22

30

50

100

Smutty Nose
Island

213

27

125

U S COAST GUARD
RESERVATION

×135

Lighthouse

Radio Tower
Causeway

Monhegan

100

White
Head
55

Manana
Island

15

12

54

Monhegan Harbor

Monhegan Island

60

126

254

107

260

132

100

Burnt
Head

Lobster
Cove

×118

30

Norton
Ledge

Lobster Point

16

60

Christmas
Cove

Rikki lives on Monhegan Island. She and her husband built their home and lived there with her family without electricity for many years. As a result of her concern for her family's diet, she began to study food and nutrition, and to forage, grow, and prepare her own whole foods. She is the author of *A Foraging Vacation, Edibles from Maine's Sea and Shore.*

"*Growing stuff in the natural state as well as what we plant in gardens is pretty pure and is kissed by salt air, which is a wonderful way to enhance flavor.*

As a child my love of the earth came from my grandfather most directly. We were taught the respect of humus and earthworms. You notice I said earth not dirt; a lot of people say dirt. It's not dirt. My grandfather scolded me one time, he said, 'no no no, this is earth, life comes from this, this is not dirt.'"

RIKKI BOEHMER

OVERLOOKING BURNT HEAD

FORAGING IN LOBSTER COVE

GAIL EDWARDS

I think of myself like a dandelion root, very deeply planted here.

Gail lives in Athens. She is the founder of Blessed Maine Herb Farm where she grows over an acre of medicinal herbs. She offers apprenticeships and classes and also makes her garden available to the public. Gail is a highly knowledgeable herbal educator, and author of *Opening Our Wild Hearts to the Healing Herbs.*

"*I very distinctly remember sitting on the back of a pickup truck...and there was absolutely nothing around...no other neighbors in any of these houses. It seemed so isolated and so alone, and I felt, ah, totally abandoned. And I just thought to myself what am I ever gonna do here. And right then, I heard this voice in my head, and it said so crystal clear to me, 'relax, you're gonna love it.'*

Eventually, I came to feel that I had come to this piece of land almost like an arranged marriage...I really didn't choose it, but I deeply fell in love with it over time."

GAIL EDWARDS

The Sacred Spring

IN THE CIRCLE

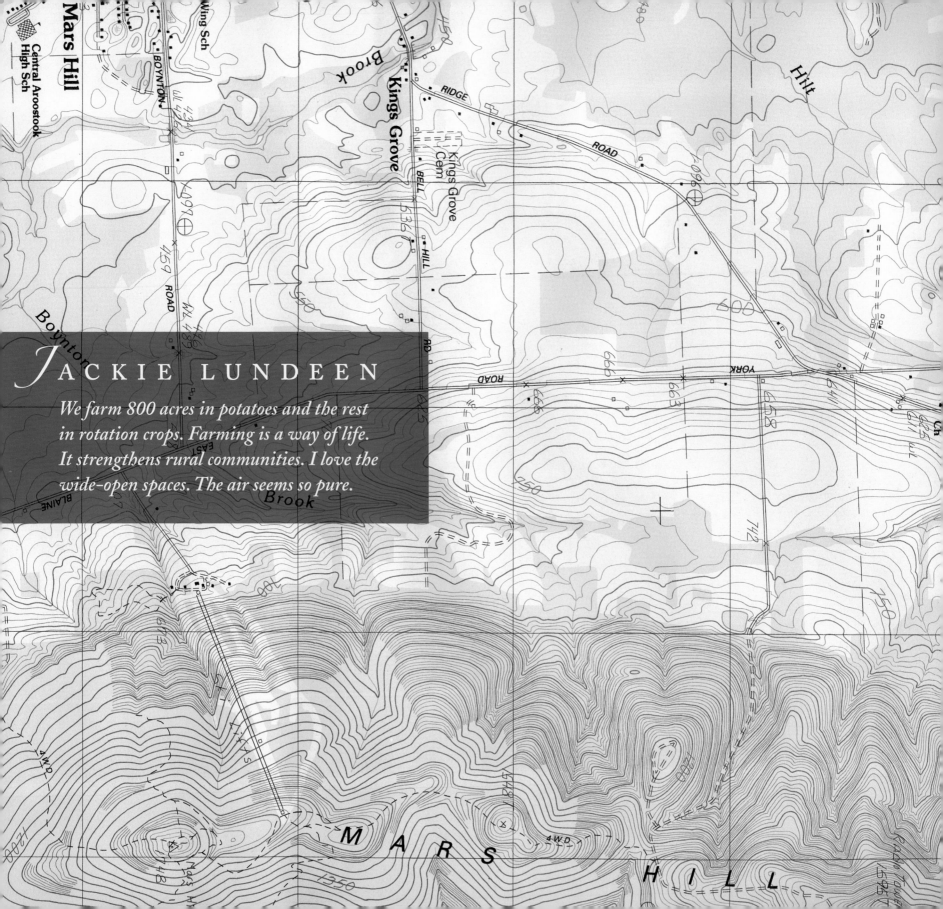

JACKIE LUNDEEN

We farm 800 acres in potatoes and the rest in rotation crops. Farming is a way of life. It strengthens rural communities. I love the wide-open spaces. The air seems so pure.

Jackie lives in Mars Hill. Her family has been farming potatoes for three generations and is one of the biggest producers in Maine. Jackie has recently become a State Representative in Augusta where she is involved in preserving the family farm and finding solutions to farming problems.

❧

"Outside is where I wanted to be, and when I get up early in the morning…the sun would be coming up, the birds would be singing, and it would be so peaceful to get on a tractor and look around as I was preparing the ground.

I'm always glad to come home. It's just a way of life for me. When I come home from Augusta…and walk across to one of our farms…200 acres across the road from where we live…I can go out there…and just stop when I want to and take a deep breath. It's just a real way of life for me."

JACKIE LUNDEEN

29

POTATO FIELD IN STORM

IN HER FIELD

CAROL VARIN

This land has supported us all these years, and it will continue to do so one way or another.

Carol lives in Beddington. She and her husband own Beddington Ridge Farm, a small diversified, family farm. She is a blueberry farmer. She also designs and sells Christmas and decorative wreaths as well as a large variety of perennials and cut flower bouquets that she takes to farmers' markets and craft shows. The Varins also run a mail order business selling their products online.

"I guess the whole thing of living in Maine probably began in my childhood when my family took camping trips to Maine and I always thought what a great place this is. So at one point we decided let's go, and we were too young and idealistic to know that you can't live off the land, so therefore, we were able to pull it off.

I don't think I'd ever want to totally give up what I have going here because I've spent my whole adult life putting it together ... so I have a lot of emotional attachment to it ... but I would love to think that whoever comes next will have their chapter to play out here, too."

CAROL VARIN

HER HOME

PICKING TOMATOES

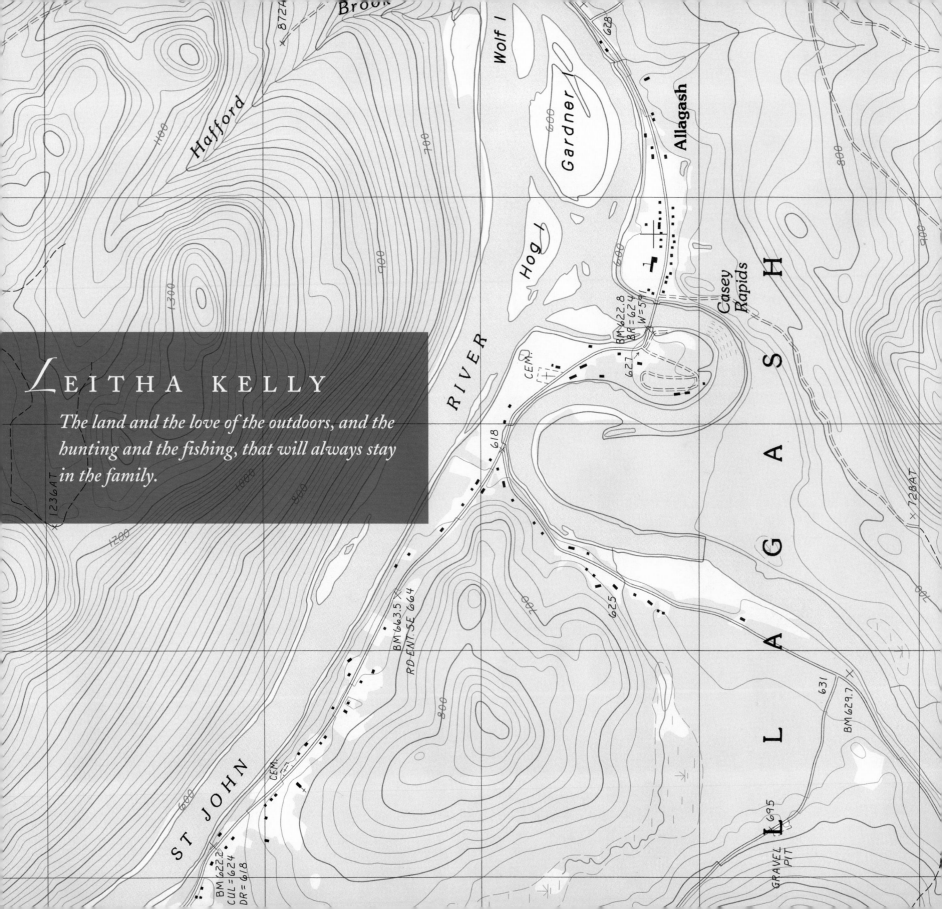

LEITHA KELLY

The land and the love of the outdoors, and the hunting and the fishing, that will always stay in the family.

Leitha lives in Allagash. Her family has been harvesting timber in the North Woods for six generations. They also work as Master Maine guides for moose, bear, deer, and fish. In addition, they host the longest dog sled race in the eastern United States. Leitha is the owner of the Two Rivers Lunch in Allagash, a family-run restaurant that is the gathering place in the town of Allagash.

"I have lived in the Allagash for sixty-three years. Both grandfathers were woodsmen. My father also was a woodsman....Never had a swimming pool, so we always swam in the Allagash River, and if we wanted to go out...to fish...you could always go out to the Allagash...it was just a peaceful way of life that I don't know that I could find anywhere else. I married Tylor in '58, his father was a woodsman, and he also was a woodsman. Then we had five children and our two older sons became woodsmen."

LEITHA KELLY

CHAIR ON THE ALLAGASH

KELLY LANDSCAPE

DEB SOULE

*By living here so long, I have made this
incredible relationship with place and land.
I wouldn't trade that for anything.*

Deb lives in Rockport. She founded Avena Botanicals, an herbal apothecary, in 1985. She is also founder of Avena Institute. Deb has been an herbalist, gardener, and wild crafter for over twenty years. Her deep love for plants and the earth inspires her gardening, teaching, and writing. She is author of *A Woman's Book of Herbs.*

"I love plants, and to be able to live and work among them every day brings incredible joy to my heart.

I could never live in the city. I have to live on the land, in the country, and feel the earth, and go barefoot in the spring and all summer, and listen to the birds return. The gardening has broadened my connection to the rhythms of life around me."

DEB SOULE

41

AVENA BOTANICAL TINCTURES

HARVESTING CALENDULAS

JENNY CIRONE

I had ten traps when I was ten. When I was thirteen, I had 145, me and my father together. I've got my license, and my boat is fixed. Chances are if I can walk, I'll be there lobstering.

Jenny lived in South Addison. The daughter of a lighthouse keeper, she trapped lobsters for over seventy-five years and also bred sheep on Nash and Little Nash Island. Her sheep were like her children, and she had a deep connection to them. Their wool is highly sought after by local weavers.

❧

"I ain't got much for home, but it is warm and comfortable, and I can, you know, do what I want to. We laid on in Jonesport either one or two weeks, before we could get on Nash Island and mind you . . . we come down there in 1916, the 16th day of January. That was the only home I ever knew, you see, because I was only three and probably didn't know much then. Here I am 91, and I don't know nothin' anyway."

JENNY CIRONE

HER HOME

FEEDING CHICKENS

MARY PHILBROOK

I knew that I was a Micmac, but what that meant as a young person, I did not know. My practice is in the native spirituality. We are caregivers.

Mary lives in Presque Isle. She is the first female Micmac Chief and was instrumental in achieving Federal Recognition of the Micmacs in 1991 with the passage of the Aroostook Band of Micmacs Settlement Act. She is very involved with serving the elders as well as the larger Micmac community and is currently the Administrative Assistant to the Aroostook Band of Micmac Council.

❧

"This is home. This is where I was born and raised. This is where I had my children. This is where my grand-children live. This is part of me. This is who I am.

This place, I think, has its own spirit. It always did as any piece of land. If you walk on a piece of property, you gotta feel it. But there is something here about the spirit; it stays here. And when you step on the ground it warms you; it comforts you. And it's saying, 'You're ok. You're ok.' I think there are a lot of different spirits here. These spirits that have come with others and stayed here because they found it comfortable."

MARY PHILBROOK

SWEAT LODGE

Micmac landscape

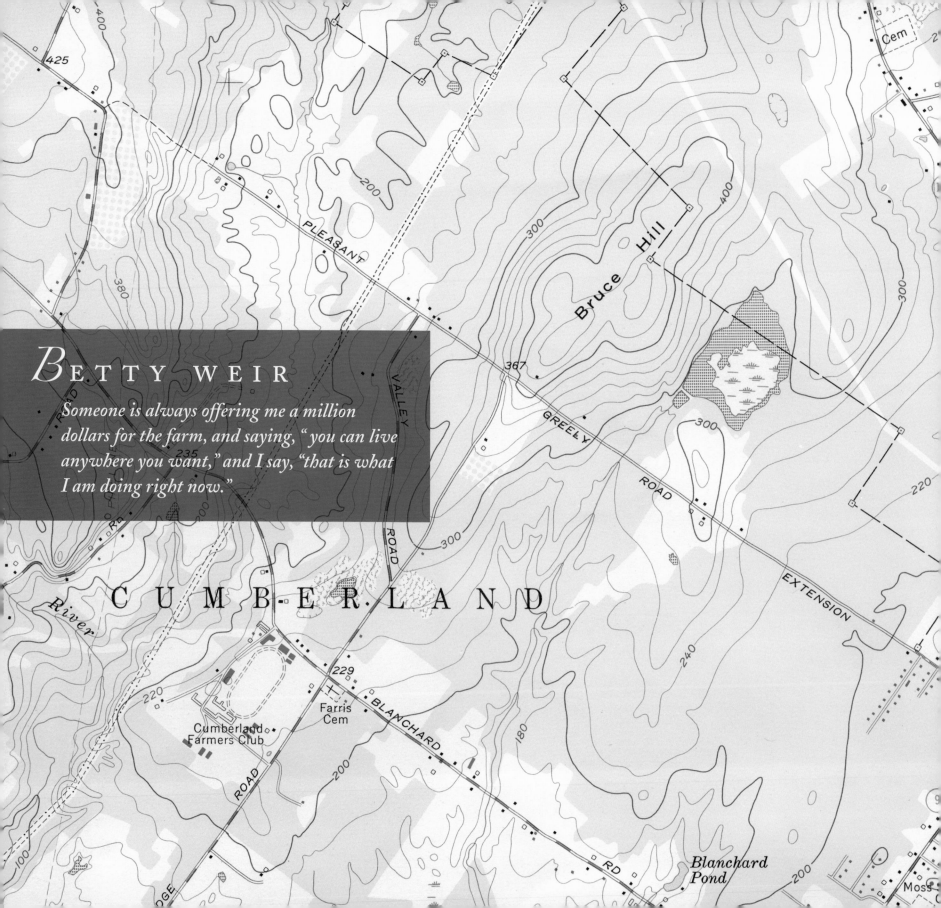

BETTY WEIR

Someone is always offering me a million dollars for the farm, and saying, "you can live anywhere you want," and I say, "that is what I am doing right now."

$\mathcal{B}etty$ lives in Cumberland. She is a diversified, organic farmer who owns Pleasant Valley Acres. She raises goats as well as beef and is also a maple syrup producer. She considers herself a steward of the land. She is one of the early members of Maine Organic Farmers and Gardeners Association.

"I've always been kind of proud, never mind that I was on a label or a farmer, I was more of a do-it-yourself person and I have always thought that we should take responsibility for ourselves.

If you go out and raise your own food and bring it in and cook for yourself.... You don't worry about self-esteem. You've got it.

It's satisfying to do something and have it real. And you wake up in the morning and its daylight, and you think wow, I made it through the night. How many old people say, 'Wow, we've got another day.'"

BETTY WEIR

THE POND

ON HER GATOR

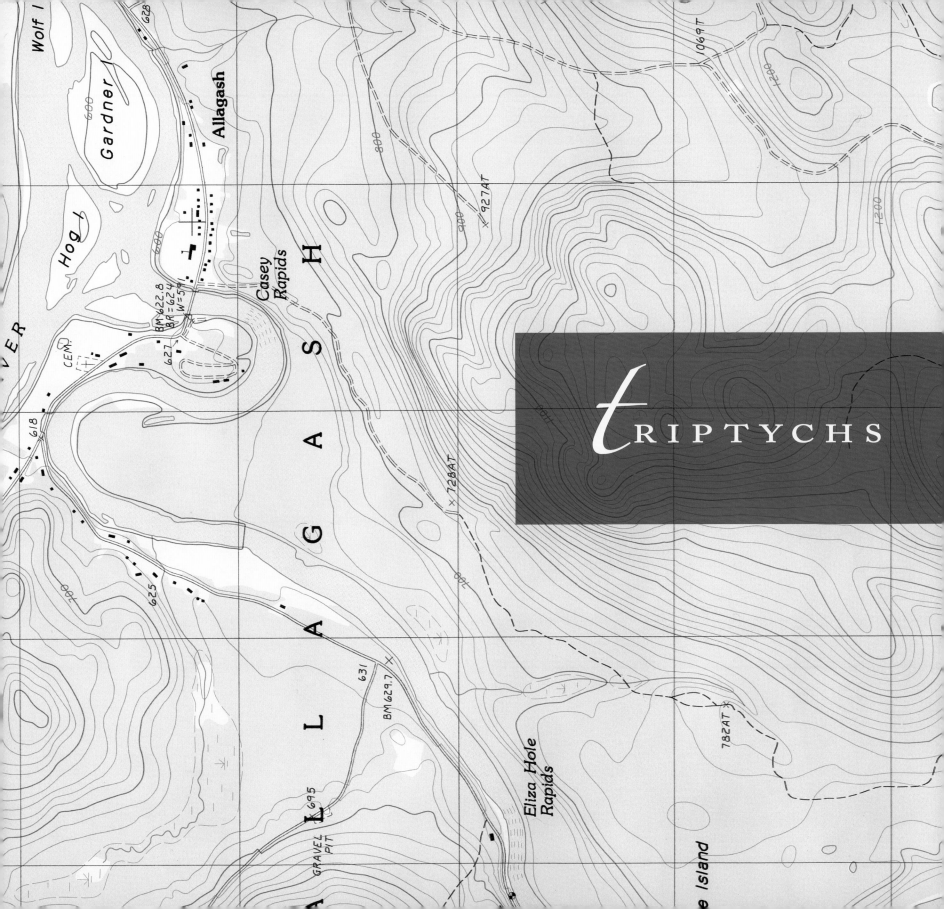

*t*RIPTYCHS

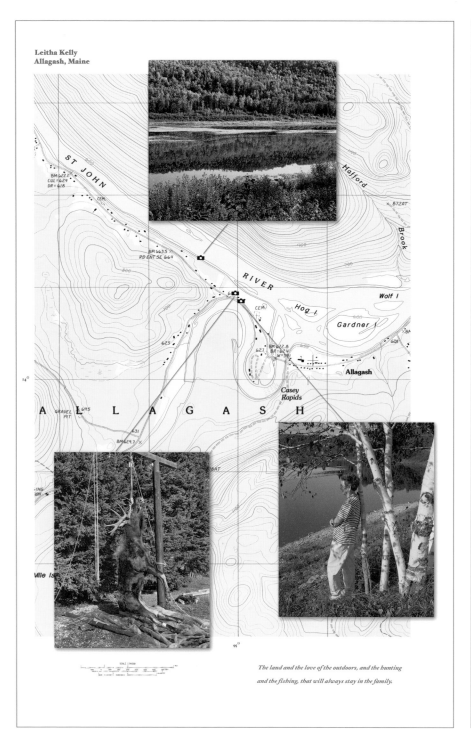

The land and the love of the outdoors, and the hunting and the fishing, that will always stay in the family.

Leitha Kelly | Allagash

I think of myself like a dandelion root, very deeply planted here.

Gail Edwards | Athens

58

Carol Varin
Beddington, Maine

BLUEBERRIES

This piece of land has supported us all these years, and it will continue to do so one way or another.

Someone is always offering me a million dollars for the farm and saying, "you can live anywhere you want." And I say, that's what I am doing right now.

Betty Weir
Cumberland, Maine

CAROL VARIN | BEDDINGTON

BETTY WEIR | CUMBERLAND

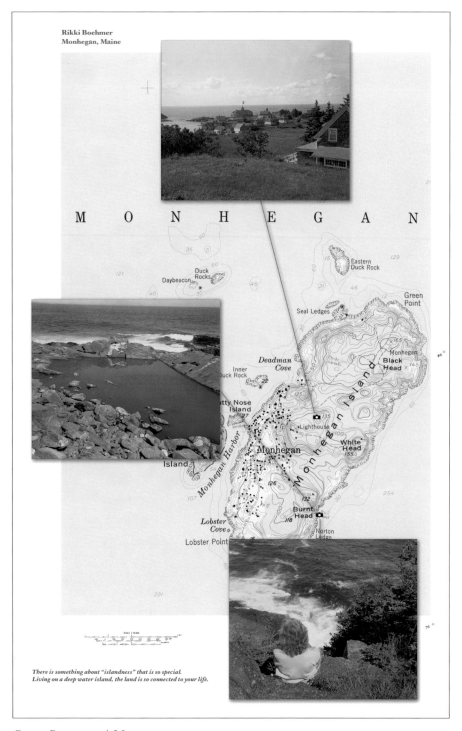

Rikki Boehmer
Monhegan, Maine

M O N H E G A N

There is something about "islandness" that is so special.
Living on a deep water island, the land is so connected to your life.

Mary Philbrook
Presque Isle, Maine

I knew I was a Micmac, but what that meant as a young person, I did not know. My practice is in the native spirituality. We are caregivers.

RIKKI BOEHMER | MONHEGAN

MARY PHILBROOK | PRESQUE ISLE

I had 10 traps when I was ten. When I was thirteen, I had 145, me and my father together.
I've got my license, and my boat is fixed. Chances are if I can walk, I'll be there lobstering.

Jenny Cirone
South Addison, Maine

Deb Soule
Rockport, Maine

By living here for so long, I have made this incredible relationship with place and land. I wouldn't trade that for anything.

JENNY CIRONE | SOUTH ADDISON

DEB SOULE | ROCKPORT

CHECKLIST

GAIL IN HER GARDEN

Rikki Boehmer

Rikki Boehmer (Raquel), Monhegan, Maine, 2001, archival ink-jet print, 20 x 16"

Foraging in Lobster Cove, 2004, archival ink-jet print, 15 x 12"

Lobster Cove, 2003, archival ink-jet print, 15 x 12"

Rikki's Hammock, 2003, archival ink-jet print, 15 x 12"

Triptych: Rikki Boehmer, Monhegan, 2003, photo collage, 49 x 33"

Gail Edwards

Gail Edwards, Athens, Maine, 2001, archival ink-jet print, 20 x 16"

The Sacred Spring, 2004, archival ink-jet print, 15 x 12"

In the Circle, 2004, archival ink-jet print, 15 x 12"

Gail with Her Dog, Lily, 2004, archival ink-jet print, 15 x 12"

Harvesting Roses, 2004, archival ink-jet print, 15 x 12"

Triptych: Gail Edwards, Athens, 2003, photo collage, 49 x 33"

Jenny Cirone

Jenny Cirone, South Addison, Maine, 2001, archival ink-jet print, 20 x 16"

Her Home, 1996, archival ink-jet print, 15 x 12"

Feeding Chickens, 1996, archival ink-jet print, 15 x 12"

Jenny Feeding Bread to Her Sheep, 2003, archival ink-jet print, 15 x 12"

Nash Island Lighthouse, 2003, archival ink-jet print, 15 x 12"

Jenny's Memorial Sign for Her Sheep, 1996, archival ink-jet print, 15 x 12"

Triptych: Jenny Cirone, South Addison, 2003, photo collage, 49 x 33"

Deb Soule

Deb Soule, West Rockport, Maine, 2004, archival ink-jet print, 20 x 16"

Avena Botanical Tinctures, 2002, archival ink-jet print, 15 x 12"

Deb Weeding, 2004, archival ink-jet print, 15 x 12"

Avena Dog, 2000, archival ink-jet print, 15 x 12"

Triptych: Deb Soule, West Rockport, 2003, photo collage, 33 x 49"

Leitha Kelly

Leitha Kelly, Allagash, Maine, 2002, archival ink-jet print, 20 x 16"

Chair on the Allagash, 2003, archival ink-jet print, 15 x 12"

Looking Out on the River, 2001, archival ink-jet print, 15 x 12"

Log Trailer in the North Woods, 2003, archival ink-jet print, 15 x 12"

Triptych: Leitha Kelly, Allagash, 2003, photo collage, 49 x 33"

Jackie Lundeen

Jackie Lundeen, Mars Hill, Maine 2003, archival ink-jet print, 20 x 16"

Potato Field in Storm, 2003, archival ink-jet print, 15 x 12"

In Her Potato Field, 2001, archival ink-jet print, 15 x 12"

Triptych: Jackie Lundeen, Mars Hill, 2003, photo collage, 49 x 33"

Mary Philbrook

Mary Philbrook, Presque Isle, Maine: 2003, archival ink-jet print, 20 x 16"

Mary and Her Mother, 1996, archival ink-jet print, 15 x 12"

Boys at Powwow, 2003, archival ink-jet print, 15 x 12"

Micmac Nation Flag, 2003, archival ink-jet print, 15 x 12"

Triptych: Mary Philbrook, Presque Isle, 2003, photo collage, 33 x 49"

Carol Varin

Carol Varin, Beddington, Maine: 2003, archival ink-jet print, 20 x 16"

Picking Tomatoes, 2003, archival ink-jet print, 15 x 12"

Her Home, 2003, archival ink-jet print, 15 x 12"

Harvesting Blueberries, 2003, archival ink-jet print, 15 x 12"

Triptych: Carol Varin, Beddington, 2003, photo collage, 33 x 49"

Betty Weir

Betty Weir, Cumberland, Maine, 2003, archival ink-jet print, 20 x 16"

Gardening with Shadow, 2003, archival ink-jet print, 15 x 12"

Betty's Grandson in Tree, 2003, archival ink-jet print, 15 x 12"

On Her Gator, 2003, archival ink-jet print, 15 x 12"

Triptych: Betty Weir, Cumberland, 2003, photo collage, 33 x 49"

Sylvia Holbrook

Sylvia Holbrook, New Vineyard, Maine, 2001, archival ink-jet print, 20 x 16"

Front Steps, 2004, archival ink-jet print, 15 x 12"

Sylvia with Her Dog and Cats, 2004, archival ink-jet print, 15 x 12"

The Barn, 2004, archival ink-jet print, 15 x 12"

Triptych: Sylvia Holbrook, New Vineyard, 2003, photo collage, 49 x 33"

BOYS AT POWWOW

NASH ISLAND LIGHTHOUSE

Lauren Shaw received her MFA in photography from the Rhode Island School of Design where she studied with Harry Callahan and Aaron Siskind. She is an Associate Professor at Emerson College, where she has been on the faculty since 1972. She is currently head of the photographic program in the Department of Visual and Media Arts. Shaw is a member of the Steering Committee of New England Women in Photography and is actively involved in educational programming for the organization. She was the recipient of the Excellence in Photographic Teaching Award from the Santa Fe Center for Photography, and has been the recipient of two regional grants from the National Endowment for the Arts and six Emerson College Faculty Advancement Fund grants. Shaw's photographs have been exhibited widely throughout the United States and are a part of the photographic collections of the Getty Museum; Museum of Fine Arts, Boston; Fogg Museum, Harvard University; High Museum of Art, Atlanta; Art Institute of Chicago; and The Library of Congress, among other institutions.